HideCrafts™

Index

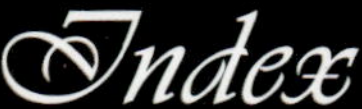

Hide preparation:

Projects:

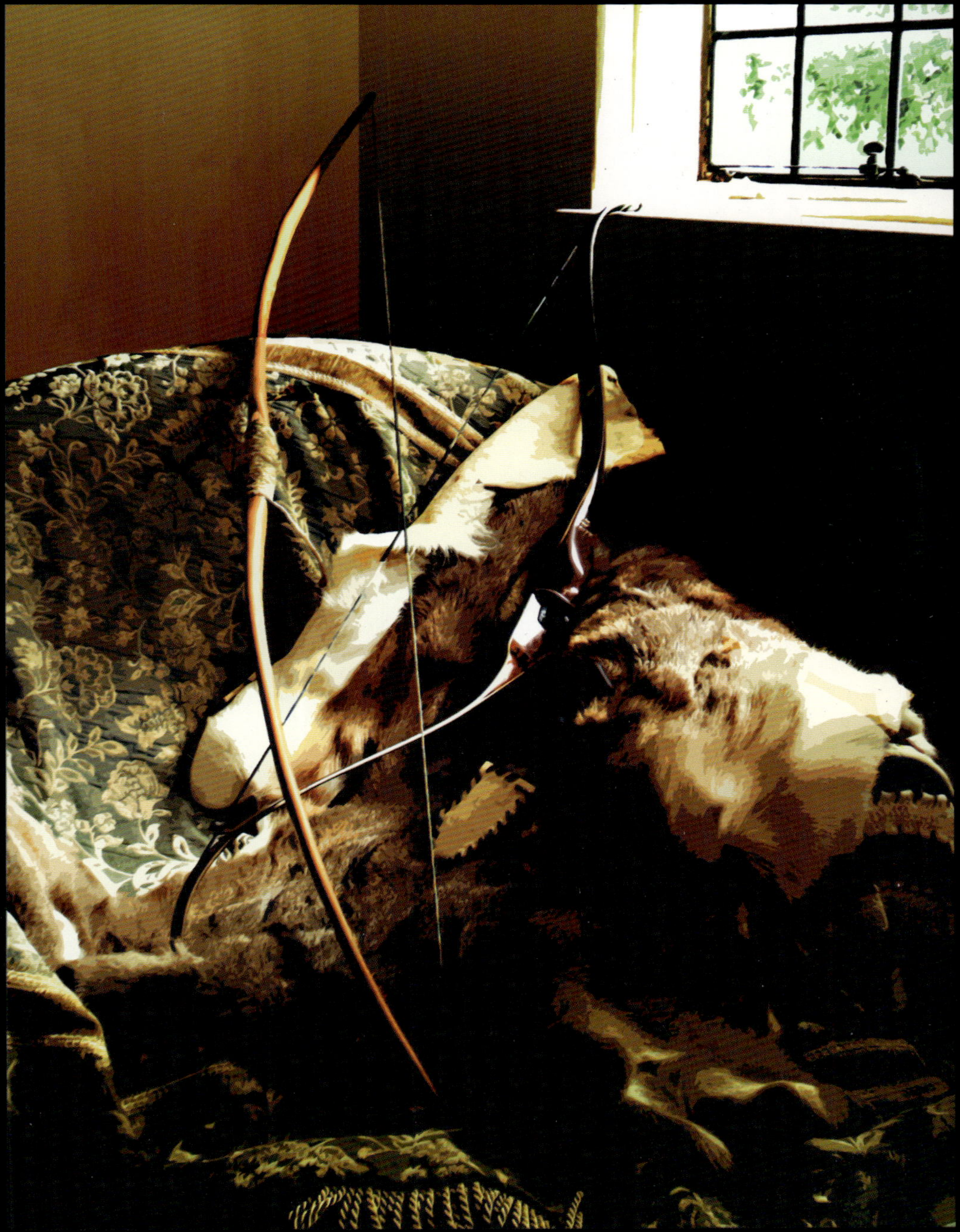

I attended graduate school in St. Louis in the mid-1990's. Cahokia Mounds, the vast complex of dirt pyramids and the center of Mississippi Valley Indian culture, was a mere 20 minutes from my apartment and had just received a brand new visitors center to the tune of several million dollars. Eager to distract myself from my studies, I made a trip over one Saturday afternoon. Even before I entered the museum, on the parking lot and sidewalks around the building I saw painted outlines of the foundations to structures that were uncovered as the museum had been built. In some places, foundations overlapped two and three times as the area had been inhabited for hundreds and hundreds of years. Once inside, I was completely transported to the world in which the Native Americans had dwelt by the realistic and vivid displays. Every aspect of their life was shown, from cradle to grave. Tools, hunting techniques, home building, were amongst the dozens of skills explained. One display I remember distinctly showed the many ways in which the indians used deer. Deer, it explained, provided everything from meat to clothes to tools to moccasins to fishing lures and more. There was very little waste. I compared this to my own deer hunting experience, which usually involved stripping the hide off of the deer (which just seemed to be in the way of the venison), cutting the meat off and then throwing the rest of the deer into the woods. What a waste, I thought. That visit to the museum stuck with me and the next fall I began to experiment with deerhide. That trip to Cahokia Mounds ultimately led to the creation of this book.

Jeff DeBruine

So many people bring home a deer during hunting season and admire the hide and wish they could do something with it but they lack the knowledge or experience. When the green hide is stretched and scraped it has a wonderful, pliable feeling, like nice leather. However, when it dries, it almost has the consistency of cardboard. Most hunters give up the idea of making something out of the hide because it appears like plenty of work with no prospect for salvaging something nice looking or useful. They end up throwing away one of the best parts of the deer. That is where this book comes in. Every project in it takes as a starting point a stiff piece of rawhide. From there we show you how to make a fun and practical article with your own hands and the help of some common woodworking tools.

The alternative to making something from the rawhide is to have your hide tanned professionally. This process takes months and sometimes(in my experience) years, and not always to your satisfaction. I've had tanned hides returned to me that were supposed to have the hair on and found that 1/3 of the hair had come off during the process. Then when your hide comes back, it is usually pretty to look at and will fit in nicely hanging over a chair or couch, but it just lies there. In this book, we'll show you how to make something useful and nice looking without having to send it off to Timbuktu.

One thing that you should not expect from reading this book is to end up with tanned pliable leather from your deer rawhide. That can be achieved if you have your hide tanned professionally or if you follow the steps in a book on how to tan it yourself (most of those books involve brain tanning) but no such directions are given here. You will, however, end up with a useful material that can be used in a variety of applications from following the steps given below. Also, in spite of my story above about being inspired by my visit to the Cahokia Mounds museum, I make no claims at all that there is any kind of genuine Indian craft depicted in this book. I am a city boy and grew up in a household where guns and hunting were frowned upon. I actually didn't start hunting until out of college but I do think it one of the most satisfying activites I've ever taken up. All of these projects were the product of my imagination and are not based on any original Indian designs.

Skinning the Deer

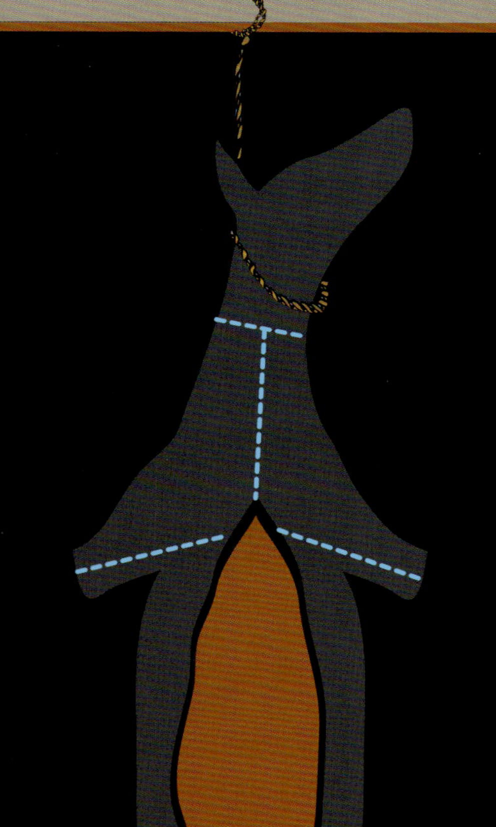

If skinning the deer is done properly, there will be no nicks, cuts, or divits out of the hide and there will be a small amount of meat left on it. If done improperly, it can cut down on the amount of usable hide you'll end up with. The goal is to end up with as large of a hole-free piece of raw-hide as you can get (although you will end up with bullet or arrow holes, unless your deer was hit by a car).

1. Hang the deer by the neck from a high place (tree, garage rafters, swing set, etc.), so that the neck of the deer is eye-level with you.

2. Cut through fur in a line around the neck at a spot about halfway between the shoulder and ears. Cut deep enough until you see muscle.

3. Assuming you've already field dressed the deer, cut up through the fur from the highest point that the cut was made in the chest cavity until you reach the cut around the neck.

4. Cut off the legs at the middle joint(I use garden lopping shears).

5. For each leg, cut the fur in a line from the belly straight out to the end of the sheared off leg.

6. Start cutting down from the cut in the neck and pulling the hide as you go. Use a sharp knife but don't make long, deep cuts. Instead, make small cross cuts and pull the hide hard with one hand as you go. You will find that you are doing more to remove the hide with your pulling hand than with your knife, because much of the hide separates from the body without even being cut. You will get to places where the muscle is stubborn and cannot be separated, especially along the deer's back. It is OK to leave some muscle on the hide.

7. When you get to the front legs, you need to do more cutting and less pulling. The skin adheres to the muscle pretty well around the legs, at times.

8. Once you have gone beyond the front legs, some people "drive" it off. Wrap a rock about as big as your fist on the fur side of the shoulder hide that is hanging down. Then tie the end of a long piece of rope around the wrapped rock. Now attach the rope to something (an ATV, riding lawn mower, car bumper, etc.) and you can pull the skin right off the rest of the deer and save yourself some effort, although you'll need to go slowly and cut through some muscle if a large section of muscle starts to pull off with the hide.

9. If you don't do step 8 then just continue by hand.

Framing the Hide

The skinned green hide will have the fur on one side and some meat and membrane on the other. There is absolutely no problem with leaving meat and membrane on the hide as this will scrape off easily in the next section. Better to leave too much on than to gouge the hide and make holes. Proceed to framing or put in plastic bag and place in freezer until convenient to do so. Hides go bad fairly quickly in warm weather and will begin to smell dreadful, rendering it unusable.

Materials

Start this step off by getting four 6 foot 2 x 4's and eight sets of nuts and bolts which are long enough to go through both 2 x 4's. You'll want to first lay the 2 x 4's on the ground in a square with corners overlapping. Then bring the 2 x 4's on the left and right each in towards the center about a foot. Drill two holes in each corner and put the nuts and bolts in place. Keep the overlap on the top and bottom pieces (i.e. don't cut off the overlap) because most likely you'll be doing this outside and it will help keep the frame from flipping over in the wind. What's also good about this setup is that you can drill several sets of holes all along the 2 x 4's so that you can make the frame as large (or small) as you want it. Also, when the last hide is scraped for the season, take out the bolts and store everything in a convenient stack in your garage until next year.

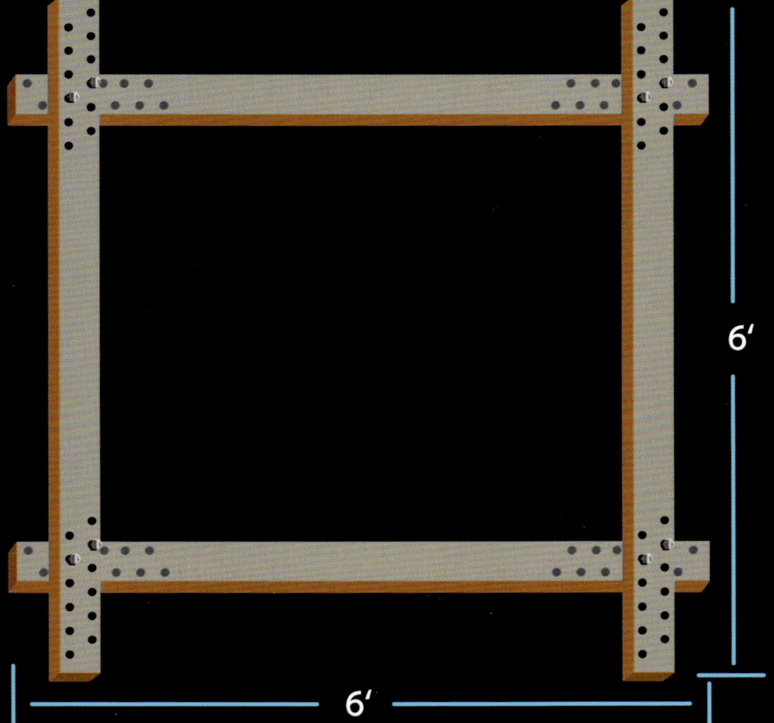

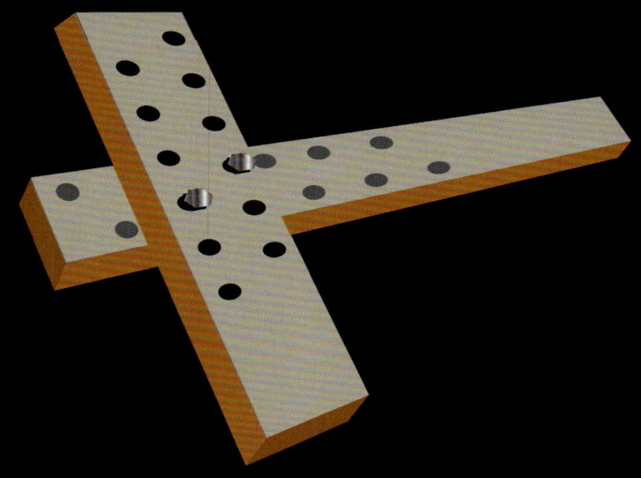

Directions

1. Lay out the frame on the ground.

2. Lay out the hide within the space of the frame.

3. Pull the hide out to the maximum it can stretch in any direction and make sure that it is still inside the frame; Adjust as necessary.

4. Poke holes through the hide all the way around, about an inch away from the edge and about every 3 inches. Use an awl, sharp nail, or something else that can poke through the green hide.

5. Use a sturdy string, like baling twine, to lace it up on the frame. Use one long piece for each of the four sides, tying it loosely at first and then tightening it up when all of the sides have been laced. Stretch it out fairly tight, but the danger here is to rip right through the hide. The possibility of this happening is the greatest around the legs (see Hide Map pg. 15). Once the hide is stretched proceed straight to scraping.

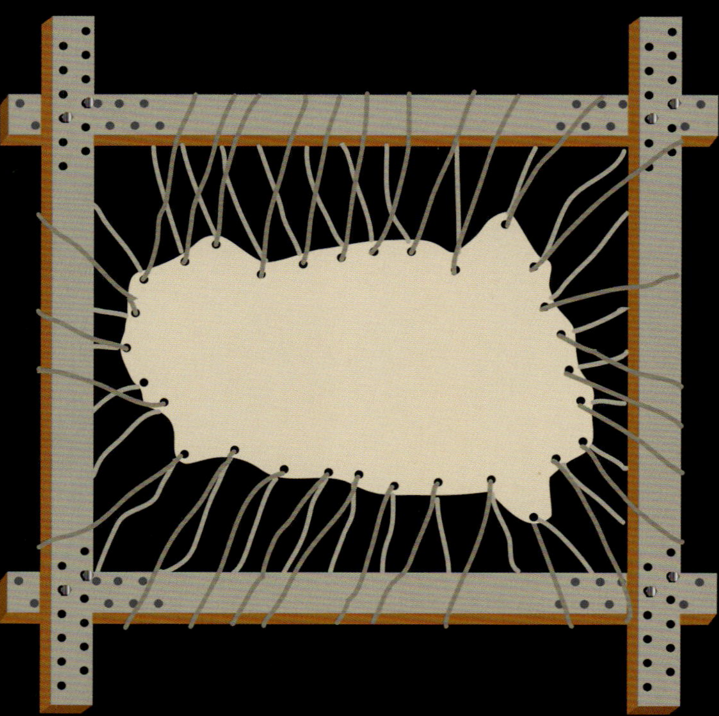

Redneck Shortcut

If you don't have the time or inclination to make a frame out of 2' x 4's, then this is the next best thing. Take a 4' x 4' pallet and nail the edges of the hide to the outside of the pallet frame on the under side, so that the hide is suspended and you will not be scraping directly against the slats. It will be rare that the size of the hide will fit exactly on the outside edge of the pallet but usually three sides will fit and the fourth edge can be nailed to the inside boards, as shown below. Scrape the hide while on the pallet and then remove the nails and reverse the hide and scrape the hair off (or remove the hide and then throw it in water and lime and let the hair fall off by itself).

Scraping

I have not included steps in this section because the goal is just to scrape away all of the meat and membrane that is between you and the actual hide. The membrane will come off in layers and you will know when you get to the hide itself because you'll reach a wall of tiny fibers that don't separate easily. The only real mistake you can make here is to slice all of the way through the hide. You need to scrape down instead of side to side. The hide is tough and will bounce back, but if you use the wrong motion it is possible to cut through it.

How to Make a Scraper

One tool that I have seen directions for in several different sources is a simple scraper (Brain Tan Buckskin by John McPherson has a very good explanation of how to make one). You don't really need a scraper, as a knife or sharpened piece of metal will do in a pinch, but the scraper with a handle makes scraping the hide worlds easier. All you really need is a piece of wood for a handle (a tree branch with a knot in it will do nicely), a piece of metal to be sharpened into a blade (an old rusty file can be ground into a strong blade), and something to bind the blade to the handle. A slot needs to be cut in the handle that will accommodate the dull end of the blade you've created and then using either raw-hide or heavy string, wrap the blade to the handle.

De Hairing

You have two choices here: 1) throwing the hide in water (or water with lime) until the hair falls off or 2) scraping the hair off with a 'scraper'. By scraping the hide off with a scraper, you would leave the hide on the frame and, using a sharp tool of one sort or another, scrape every last hair off of the hide. Obviously, it is loads easier to toss the hide in water and let the hair fall off by itself. This proceeds even faster if a cup or two of lime is added. But the hide has a different feel once it has been allowed to soak in water or water and lime, especially with lime added. The hide becomes a tad more brittle and less leatherlike. Rawhide that has just been scraped will be more forgiving and will do exactly what you want it to do. Soaked rawhide, especially the thin areas, will become more like paper and the thick parts around the middle will become more like hard cardboard. However, you can do any of the projects in this book by using rawhide prepared by either method. If the soaking method is used, linseed oil must be applied to the de-haired rawhide after it has dried.

1. Start scraping from the neck down. Don't go against the direction of the hair; it doesn't scrape off nearly as easy. Always scrape the direction of the hair and when you get to areas where the hair goes in different directions, i.e. around the legs, follow the direction of the hair. Scrape down about an inch or two each time you make a pass. You will only be scraping off an area about 1/4" - 3/8" wide each pass but that is the way it is done.

2. Be careful around the legs as the hide is weaker here and there is danger of scraping through it.

3. Without stopping it will take about 2 hours. This is the most time consuming drudge work in the whole book. Apply linseed oil with cloth or brush and allow to dry. Do this to both sides, then wipe off excess.

   Don't start the process of soaking your rawhide if the temperature is very hot (in the 90's or above). Definitely don't leave the container out in the sun. Put it in a dark cool place.

1. Find a large container which is either galvanized metal or plastic.

2. Fill the container with room temperature water (or colder) and a cup or so of lime. You can get lime at a hardware store.

3. Place the hide in the lime-water mixture and make sure it is fully submerged. I usually have to place a couple of large rocks on the hide because part of it always wants to rise above the water level.

4. Now it's time to play the waiting game. I've seen hair come off of the hide in as little as three or four days and other times it takes weeks. Temperature plays a role but it usually is just the tenacity of the hair to stick on the hide that decides how much time it will take. Just keep pulling on that hair and when it starts to slip off fairly easily all over the hide then you are ready.

5. Remove the hide from the water. Rinse it several times to get the lime water out of it.

6. Restring your hide on the frame you built earlier, using the same holes in the hide to guide the strings through.

7. Using a knife or some other like tool, scrape the hair off using the knife in a downward motion.

8. Most of the hair will come off easily. Usually, there is a small, stubborn patch of hair, often on backside of the deer, near the tail, which just doesn't want to come out. Using some sort of a cutting tool(I've used a razor blade and also electric shears for a dog) cut the hair down as near to the hide as you can. Then use a sharp knife to scrape away the remainder.

9. Let the hide dry. When it is completely dry, apply good ole' linseed oil. Apply with a rag or paint brush to both sides. Wipe off excess. Let it sit for a day or two or until it loses it's oily feel.

10. When you are ready to cut a piece of the rawhide for use in a project, cut the piece and apply mink oil liberally to the piece. Let it sit overnight and wipe off the excess the next day.

Making Walnut Stain

I am fortunate enough to have dozens of walnut trees in the vicinity of my house. Unfortunately, the walnuts in the yard have to be picked up or they will kill the grass, which is very tedious but provides me with an almost inexhiustible supply of walnut stain. There are probably dozens of ways to make walnut stain, but this is very easy and difficult to mess up:

Directions

1. Fill a five gallon bucket with very ripe walnuts (including hulls). The way to tell if they are ripe is to roll one under your feet and if the green hull comes off rather quickly and the inside is a gooey black slime covering the nut, then it's perfect. For one that is not ripe, the hull will be rather difficult to remove and the inside will be light colored and will have no dark slime in it.

2. Once the bucket is fairly full, add cold water to it. If you want a thick, dark stain, add less than a half a gallon. If you want a more diluted stain, add more than a half gallon. The water will percolate down through the walnuts, bringing with it the stain from the ones on the top down to the bottom.

3. Let it sit for a couple of days.

4. Start removing the top walnuts from the bucket by hand. When you get close to the bottom, you will come to the water level, which will be black.

5. Pour the liquid from the 5 gallon bucket into a container.

6. Strain the mixture to remove particles. I use an old kitchen strainer we keep in the garage.

Stain is ready to use. As I said above, if you're not happy with the thickness, use different amounts of water or let some of the water evaporate.

Other Types of Natural Stains

Besides walnut stain, there are a variety of natural stains available and the ingredients of many are as easily obtainable as walking out in the woods and gathering berries or bark. Blackberries are the most common thing to make stain out of in my area, besides walnuts. As anyone who has accidentally spilled some fresh blackberry juice on a clean, white t-shirt would know, blackberries make a terrific stain. The way to extract the juice is to boil a pot full of berries and stir it continuously so as not to burn the bottom. When the mixture has broken down the blackberries completely, take the pot off of the stove. Run the mixture through a strainer and let the liquid cool completely and you are ready to stain the rawhide. The resulting stain will leave a blackish/dark blue finish on the dyed rawhide lace. Raspberries (if you would be prepared to sacrifice them for this endeavor) can also be used and would be prepared in the same manner as the blackberries. The resulting stain leaves a very interesting dark red on the lace. Various types of bark can also be used to create stain. I used apple wood once, and let the bark sit in a bucket of cold water for a couple of weeks. The dye, however, is not very concentrated so you need to use a lot of bark for just a little water; Experiment with what you have in your area.

Making Lace

All of the projects that I have in the book use a dyed lace made out of rawhide tinted with walnut stain. The lace really makes the projects more attractive because it provides a color contrast to the rawhide and also gives it an attractive pattern. Making the lace is not hard but the steps must be followed or you'll end up with a brittle, patchy string of rawhide.

Directions

1. Cut the length of lace you'll need from the hide, making it 1/4" inch wide and however long it will be. To make it even and consistent, use a ruler or yard-stick and make sure it is evenly 1/4" the whole length. Also try not cut it from the very thin areas of the hide, i.e. near where the legs join the main hide; (See Hide Map section).

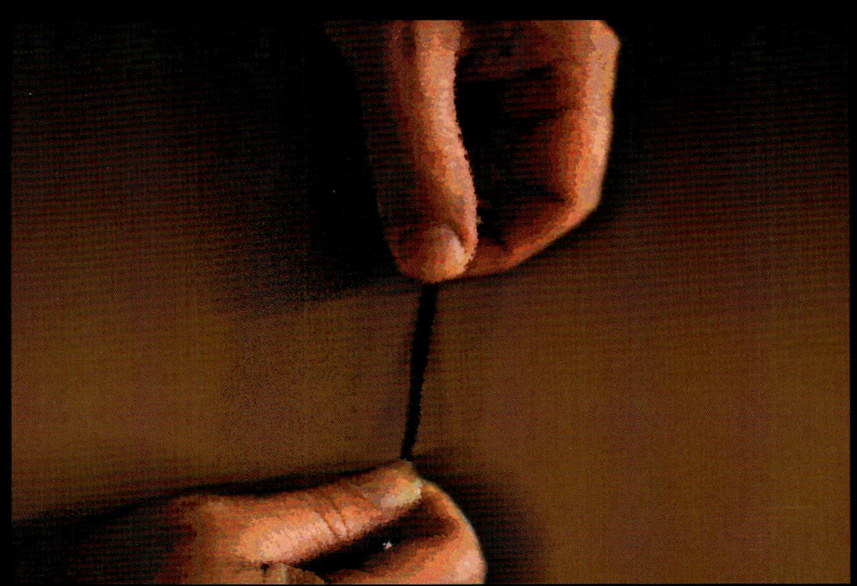

2. Soak the lace in the dye overnight. I use natural walnut stain from walnuts I have gathered in our yard. See the Making Walnut Stain section to make walnut stain.

3. Fish the lace out of the container of dye and, using paper towels, pat it dry.

4. Let the lace dry on some newspaper for about an hour, hour and a half, and make sure that it is flat and NOT twisted and NOT in the sun.

5. Pat the lace dry again, this time firmly with paper towels. Starting at one end, grab the lace with both hands (between thumb and forefinger) about 2 or 3 inches apart, stretch the lace about a half an inch or more. Move your hands down to the next point where you left off and continue doing this all the way down the lace. The idea is to stretch the rawhide lace out because it will have soaked up a lot of water and fattened up. You can't just hold on to both ends and pull because some areas are weaker than others and it would not stretch evenly. If you see a section

that looks weaker or is thinner than the rest, don't stretch it as much. The goal here is to get a piece of lace that is uniform in width.

6. Once the stretching is done, get some mink oil between your fingers and apply liberally to both sides of the lace. While you are applying this, make sure you bend the rawhide well to work the mink oil in the lace. This gives it a supple feel. Wipe off excess and it's ready to use.

   If you let the lace dry completely before applying mink oil, it will turn brittle and be difficult to soften up.

Making a Needle

To easily thread the lace through the rawhide, you'll need to make a small needle out wood/plastic/whatever. I used hard maple because it just doesn't split. Bellow is an Illustration of what your needle should look like.

Or you might use a traditional metal leather needle.

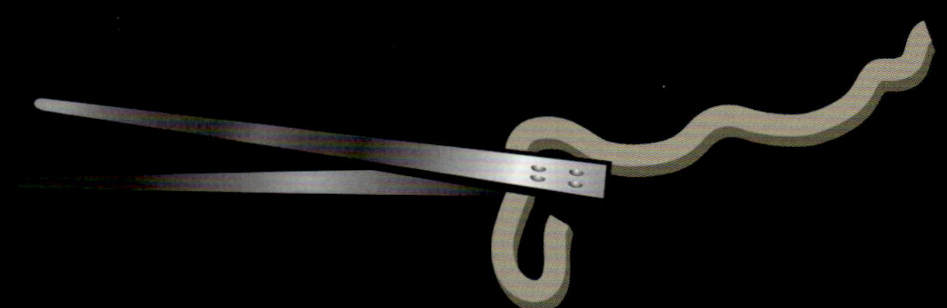

Using an Awl

There are two ways to easily make holes in rawhide for threading a lace. One way involves using a power drill and the other involves an awl. With the power drill, you just select a bit that is close in size to the lace that you are making and mark your holes in the rawhide and drill away. Very simple, and you are left with nice looking, uniform, round holes. The awl is harder to use, creates more possibility of injury, and doesn't make as uniform of a hole as a drill. However, the awl is mostly what I use when sewing my rawhide together. The awl makes a slice in the rawhide which the lace can easily pass through and doesn't leave any extra open space like the power drill holes do. The lace just disappears into the rawhide for a cool effect that can't be done with the power drill. That being said, the awl does weaken the rawhide more than the drill. The reason is that the awl starts a cut in one direction of the hide when it is pushed all of the way through. By starting a cut in one direction, the rawhide will have more of a tendency to tear in that direction if it is stressed The power drill removes all of the fiber by creating a round hole but doesn't start a slash in any particular direction. If you're looking for an awl, most decent swiss army knifes have one and that is what I use.

Shaded and dotted area shows an area of the hide that is thinner and weaker than the greater portion of the hide. When cutting a portion of the hide for a project keep this in mind.

A Note about Bullet and Arrow Holes:

Most of your hides will have a big fat bullet hole or arrow cuts right in the middle of the hide, prime real estate. This is not necessarily bad. You can incorporate this into your project if you plan properly. I made a quiver with a bullet hole very close to the opening of the quiver and put a piece of lace through it to use as a shoulder strap.

Arm Guard

If a bow is part of your arsenal you may wish to make an arm guard to accompany the practice quiver. This easy project is also a good one for when you don't have a lot of hide left to work with.

Materials

1. Pieces of elastic string.

2. Hooks and eyes (I used Dritz brand from a sewing store).

3. A modest sized piece of deer hide.

4. Rawhide lace (see Making Lace pg. 13).

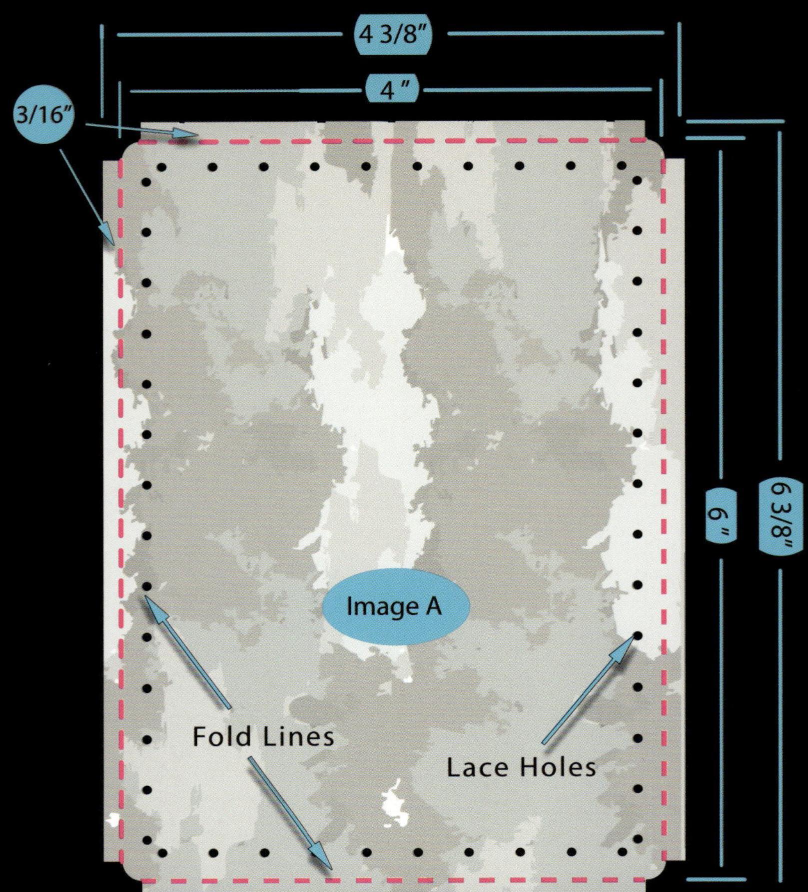

Arm Guard

Directions

1. Cut out a piece of rawhide as shown in Image A.

2. Cut each one of the corners as shown in Image B.

3. Put a coat of mink oil on both sides and then wipe off excess and let dry overnight.

4. Fold over 1/4" all the way around except at rounded corners as shown in Image C.

5. Using an awl (or drill) make holes 1/2" apart along the edge of the folded over rawhide as shown in Image A.

Cut the corners as you see in Image B.

This allows the folds to clear without crimping.

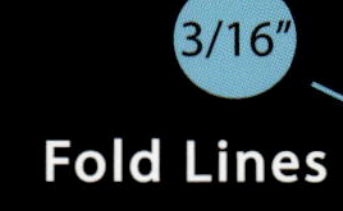

Fold Lines

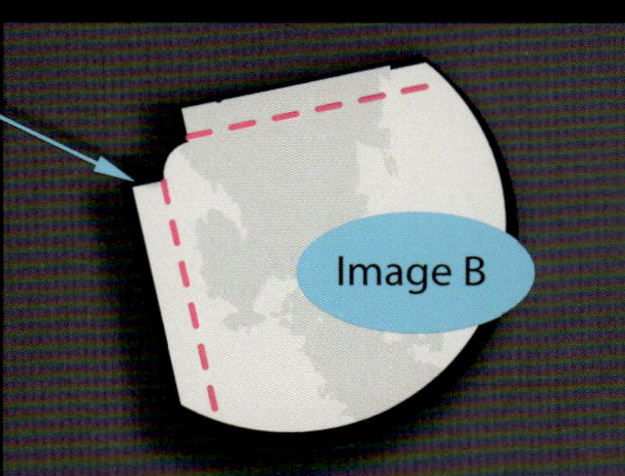

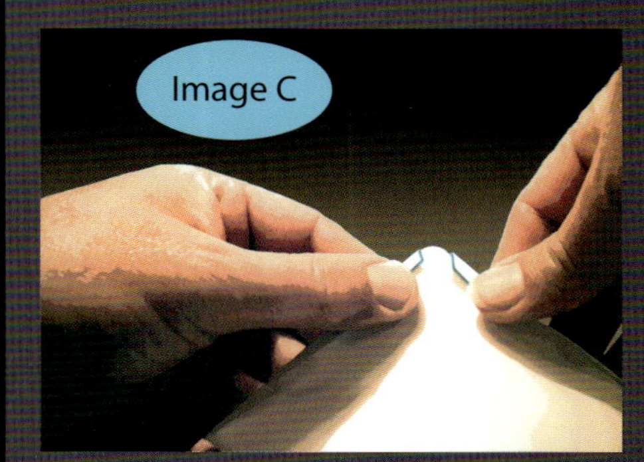

Fold the 3/16" flap over toward the back of the Arm Guard, as shown in this illustration.

6. Using dyed lace, sew all the way around the rawhide as shown in Image D.

7. Time to apply the elastic straps.

Back view of lacing for the Arm Guard.

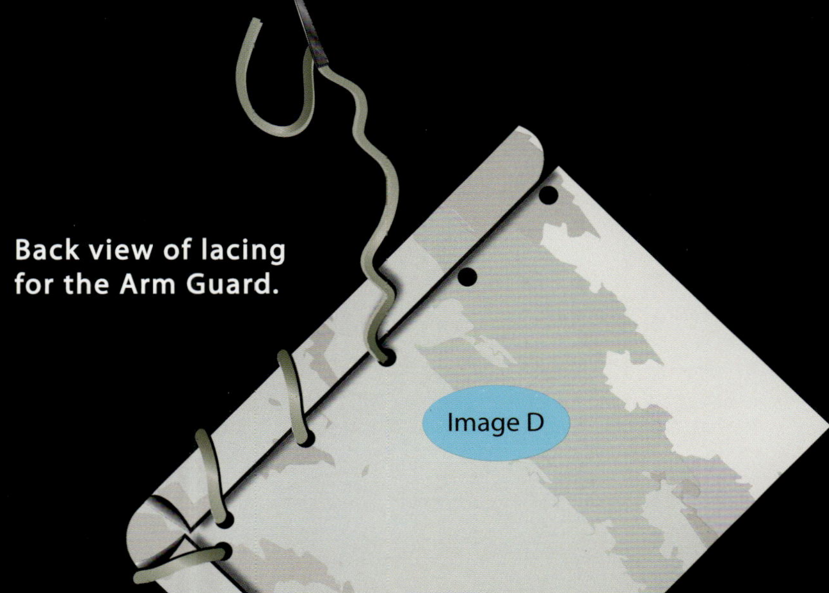

Top view showing hooks and elastic straps.

Arm Guard Elastic and Hooks

You're going to need to buy some pieces of elastic string and hooks and eyes. The covered hooks and eyes in the illustration are made by Dritz, which should be available in any fabric or sewing shop.

I applied three sets of hooks and eyes and made holes in the rawhide close to the edge and ran a small loop of lace through the holes to attach the hooks and eyes, as can be seen in the illustrations. Measure the elastic so that it fits comfortably around your arm. You may also want to take into account that you might be wearing a jacket or shirt when you are shooting your bow, so leave enough space when you cut and tie the elastic loop.

Back of guard (against arm) showing were the clips are tied off.

HideCrafts™

Wastepaper Basket

You can give your den a cabin-like feel with this deer hide waste basket. The basket can be any size you want. This is a fairly simple project that is much like the Practice Quiver in construction and shares some of the illustrations.

Materials

1. Rawhide, fairly large piece (see Image A for measurement).

2. Plenty of rawhide lace (see Making Lace pg. 13).

3. Wire coat hanger.

4. Piece of hardwood 1/2" thick and at least 6" x 6".

5. Brass or copper tacks.

Directions

1. Cut a piece of rawhide in the shape as shown in Image A. To draw this, put a brick or something heavy on a long string. Draw an arc at 27.5" and also another arc 12" beyond the first arc. This will give you a twelve inch tall waste paper basket. You can increase or decrease this according to what you want.

2. Using the awl (or electric drill), make 3 rows of holes in the hide. Make each hole 1/2" apart. The single row on the left should be 1/4" from the left edge. The two rows on the right should be 1/4" and 3/4" from the right edge.

3. Using rawhide lace, sew the two sides together with the side with the row of two holes going on the inside.

4. Measure and cut the base for this from a 6" x 6" x 1/2" piece of hardwood. Make it a perfect circle.

5. Using a power sander, sand off 1/4" all the way around the bottom of the disc but tapering off toward the top.

6. Test the bottom of the rawhide cone to see if it conforms to the disc. There should be about a half inch overlap on the rawhide. Make adjustments as necessary.

7. Pull the rawhide tightly around the disc and, using brass or copper tacks (I used nails for external use from Lowe's), pound a nail every 2" to secure the rawhide to the wooden disc.

8. Using a wire coat hanger, straighten it until it is a perfect line. You will probably need a pliers and a vice.

9. From the straightened hanger, make a perfect circle whose diameter is equal to the OUTSIDE of the top of the basket, 1/2" down from top edge. Attach the ends by bending little hooks from the ends using pliers.

10. Fold the top half inch of the basket outside over the hanger and make holes every 1/4" with awl (or drill)

11. Lace up the edge and it's done.

HideCrafts™

Wastepaper Basket

The inner arc is 27.5" from the origin and the outer arc is 39.5" from the origin. The distance from the end points on each arc are 16" and 23" (from point to point, not along the arc).

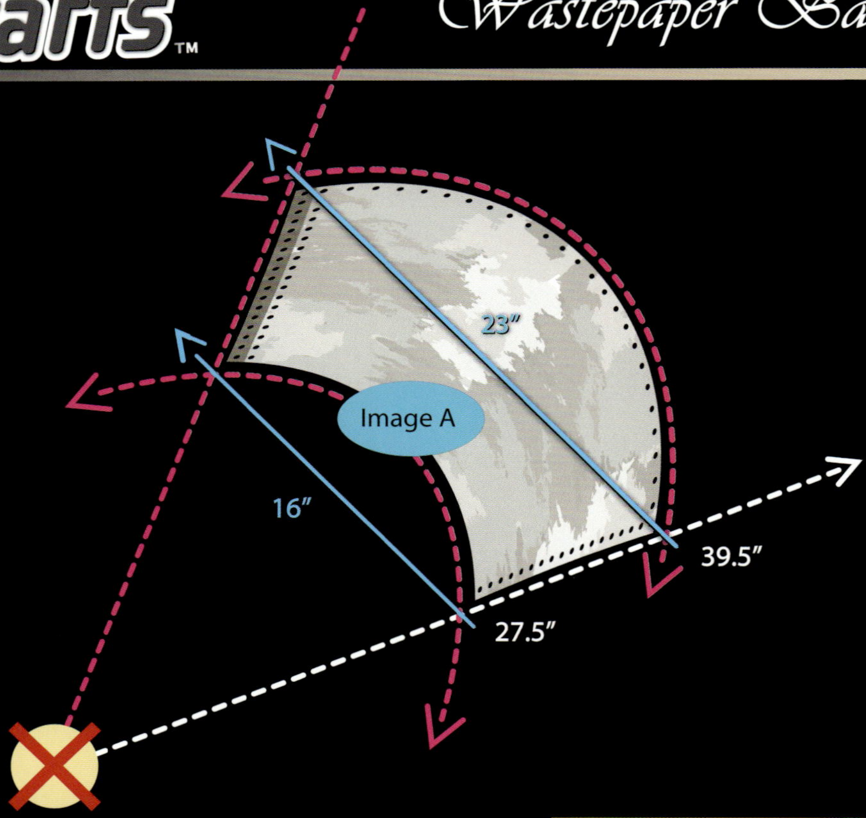

The arcs can be drawn by fixing a nail at the point of origin (red X); Then using a string and pencil to mark the arc.

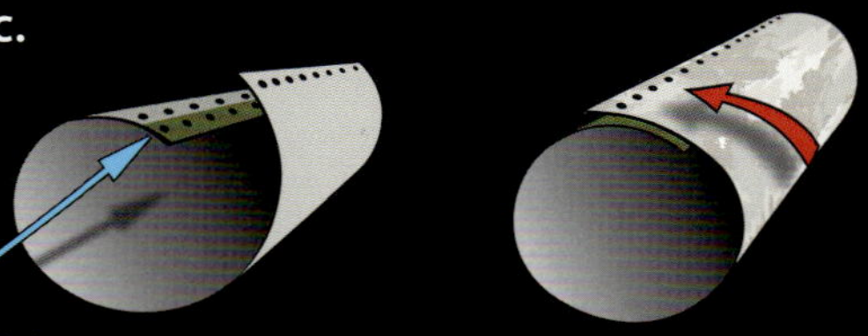

Overlap, shown in green.

Knot this end

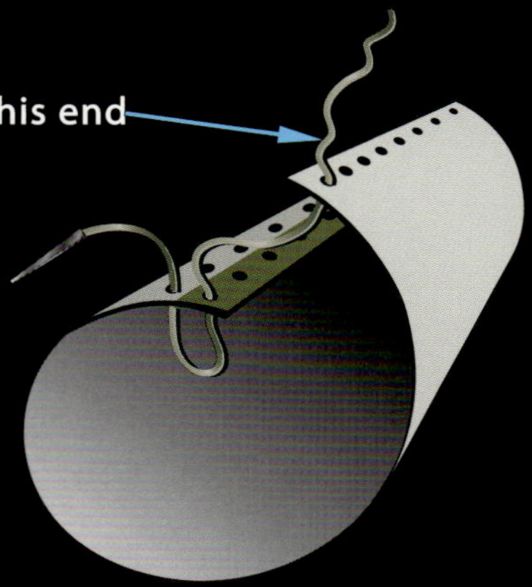

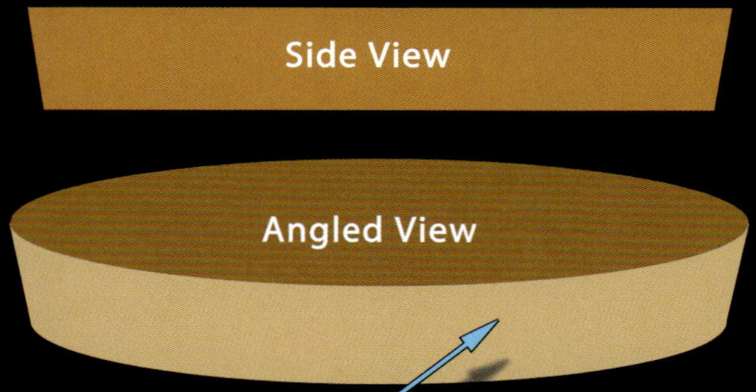

The side of the wood base is angled using a sander bit on a drill. Try to aproximate the angle of your basket. Other tools, like belt sanders, may be used if you have them.

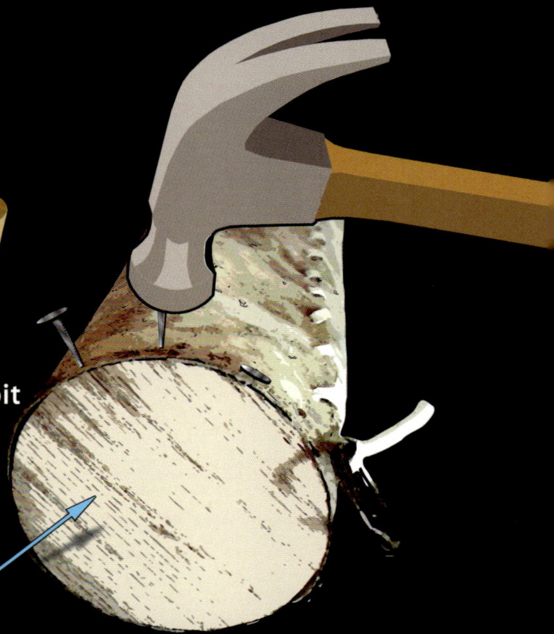

The wood base is fitted to the basket and then tacked in place as shown here.

HideCrafts™ — *Wastepaper Basket*

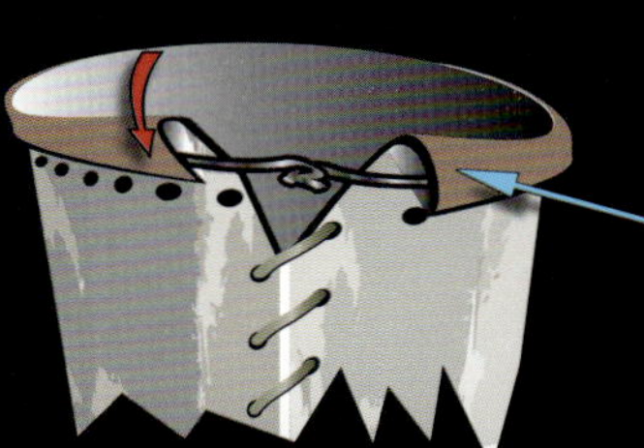

Fold the top of the basket over the wire.

Lace the top with the wire enclosed.

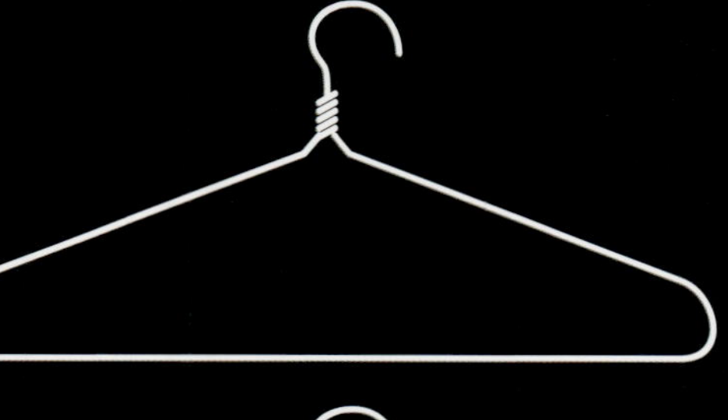

Cut the coat hanger top off with wire cutters.

This is the wire seen under the top fold.

Make bends to the hanger wire as you see here. Needlenose pliers work well for this.

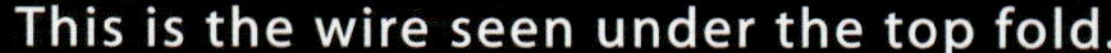

The bent wire becomes hooks that work as illustrated here.

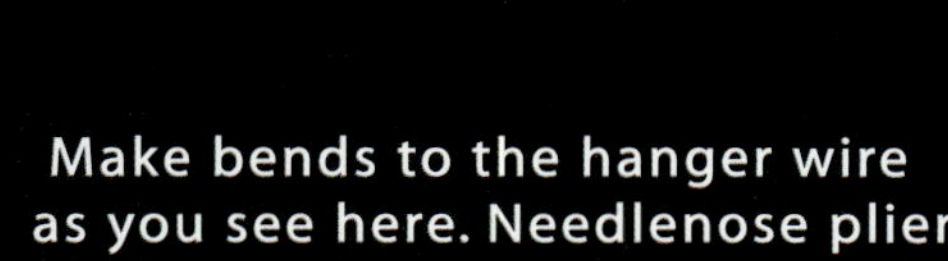

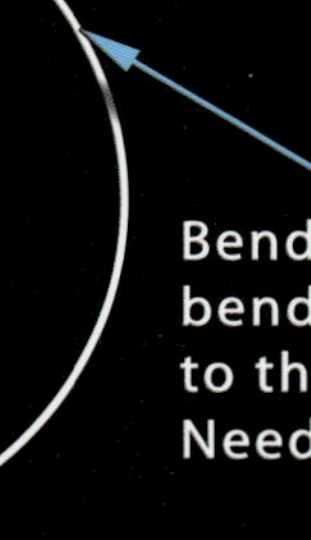

Bend the wire to a circular shape and bend hooks on the ends. Make hook bends to the ends of hanger wire as you see here. Needlenose pliers work well for this.

The fanny pack can be used for various purposes; hunting, muzzle-loader kit bag, bike riding, general use fanny pack, etc. The fanny pack is also very attractive and suitable for men and women.

Materials

1. Several pieces of rawhide of various sizes.

2. Belt buckle, small plastic clamping type.

3. Several feet of stained rawhide lace (see Making Lace section, pg. 13)

4. Metal eyelets to rivet belts to fanny pack. I use a set made by Dritz. Purchase at local sewing shop.

Directions

1. Cut pieces of rawhide according to the illustrations. Measure the belt pieces according to your waist size and add in the width of center piece (Image 1).

2. Cover the piece of rawhide with mink oil. Really rub it in. Let sit overnight.

3. Wipe off excess mink oil.

Deer Hide Fanny Pack

4. Make folds in the main piece (Image1) as shown in illustration.

5. Use an awl to make slits for attaching side pieces (Image 2) and (Image 3).

6. Use lace and needle to attach the sides (Image 2) and (Image 3) to the main body (Image 1).

7. Make two holes (Image 4) for button slit, as shown in illustration. Cut from hole to hole to make slit.

8. Use lace and needle to stitch around slit.

9. Attach piece (Image 4) to piece (Image 1) using lace.

10. Use lace and needle to stitch around edge of piece (4) so as to leave no raw edges.

Note; Black dots on images are approximate location of where to make holes with the awl. The lacing holes on each piece need to be aligned when pieces are sewn together.

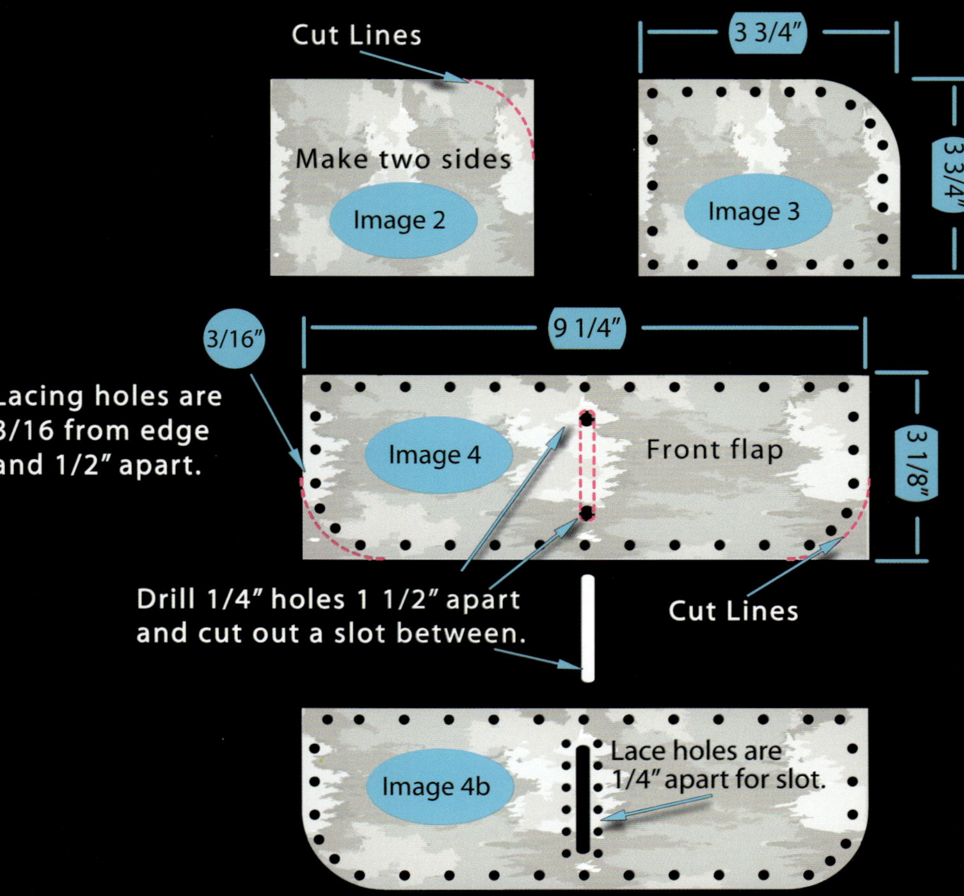

11. Attach a button to piece (Image 1) in location as shown on illustration. I used a cross section of deer antler and drilled two holes through it and then attached the button with rawhide lace and tied a knot on the inside with the lace.

12. Now it's time to make the belt. This is very similar to the guitar/mandolin strap except that you'll be making two pieces and the ends of the pieces need to accommodate a plastic belt buckle with a pinch type end.

13. The tricky part here is to attach the two belt pieces to piece (Image1). I went to a fabric store and bought an "Eyelet Kit" made by Dritz, which came with a tool to rivet the eyelets. See illustration for where to rivet belt to pack.

14. Once you have the right belt buckle see illustration for how to apply.

Almost any buckle will do, but I prefer buckles that do not require that holes be punched in the length of the belt for size adjustments. I have used a buckle that clamps to the belt.

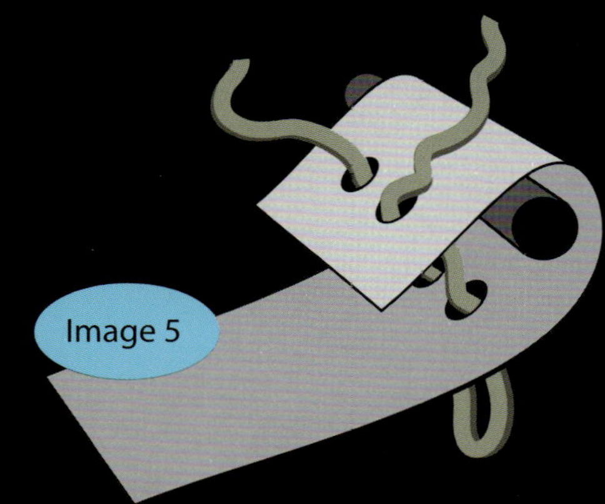

Image 5

All buckles will have a shaft or bar to fix the belt to the buckle. Images 5 and 6 show the underside of the belt and buckle where the lace that holds the buckle to the belt strap is tied off. Observe how the strap is looped around the buckles shaft from the top side to the underside of the buckle.

You will punch or drill holes in the belt as you see in image 5. The belt runs arround the buckle bar. Then the lacing runs through to the underside and is snugged and knotted.

Image 6

Underside of belt and the attached buckle.

View of the body and side panels; Showing how the straps attach to the main body of the pack

Firewood Holder

This firewood holder requires a little more woodworking tools and skills than the other projects but it is not at all beyond the range of the novice woodworker. Beyond a few straight cuts, the curved cuts on the front and back, and boring the holes for the dowels there is no other woodworking wizardy involved. In addition, the piece shown in the illustration below was made entirely from scrap pieces from the local wood shop, except for the dowels, for a total cost of less than $10. Although the holder is simple in construction, the quarter round edging on the bottom and the brass tacks give it a sophisticated look. If you want to make yours larger than what is shown in the illustration, make the dimensions of the front and back wider and there is no need to mess with the length.

Materials

1. 3/4" thick pieces of scrap of varying sizes and widths.

2. Two 20" hardwood dowels with a 5/8" diameter.

3. Two pieces of hardwood with dimensions 2" x 13 1/2" x 3/4".

4. Two pieces of hardwood with dimensions 2" x 16 1/2" x 3/4".

5. Two pieces of quarter round with length 20".

6. Two pieces of quarter round with length 18".

7. Piece of rawhide 32" x 20".

8. Rawhide lace (see Making Lace pg. 13).

9. Brass upholstery nails or tacks (I used #9 antique brass).

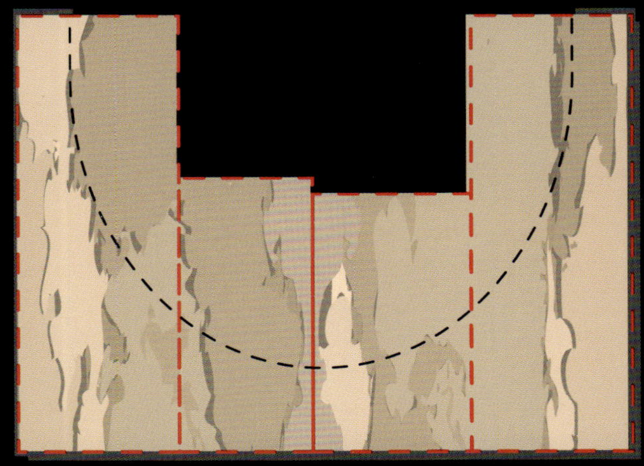

HideCrafts™

Firewood Holder

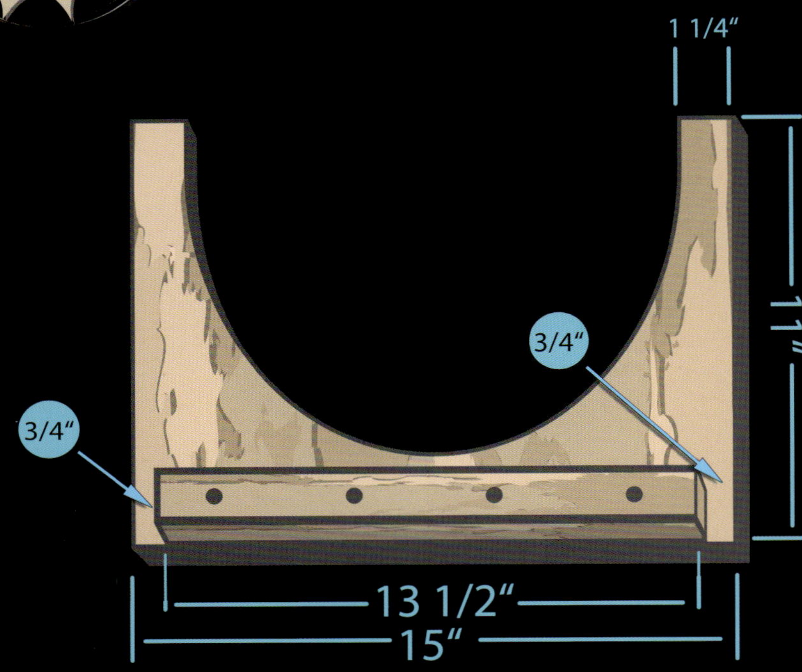

5. Glue the 18" x 5/8" dowels in place with wood glue.

6. Measure, cut, and glue the quarter round to the bottom of the holder. Get a nice sharp 45 degree on each corner.

7. The holder can now be stained.

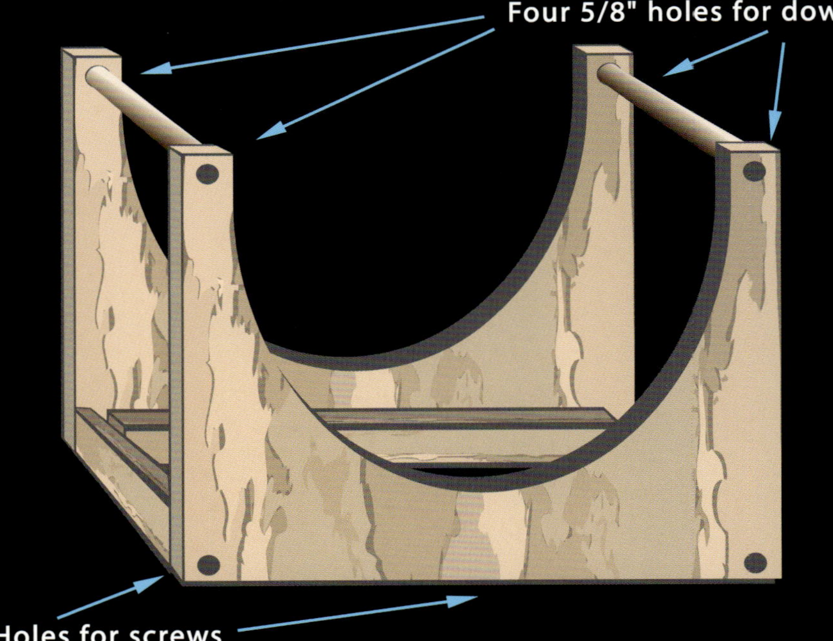

Directions

1. Using wood glue (Elmers does the trick) glue and clamp your scrap pieces together as in the illustration, so that you have enough to make the 11" x 15" dimensions. There will be two pieces, a front and back.

2. When this is dry, cut the U-shaped space out.

3. Put a 2" x 13 1/2" x 3/4" piece as a brace on the inside of the front and back. Use one screw for each piece of wood in the section. Pre-drill the holes for the screws and do not go all of the way though the wood. When placing the brace, make sure that it is exactly 3/4" from each side.

4. Route out four 5/8" holes as shown in the illustration. The center of the hole should be 1" down from the top.

8. Time to apply the rawhide. Wrap one side of the rawhide around the dowel as shown in the illustration and then draw marks every 1/2" with a pencil, about 1/2" below the bottom of the dowel. Use awl and make vertical slits. Thread the lace through the slits in the rawhide.

10. Wrap the other side around the dowel, draw guide marks, make slits with awl and then apply the lace through the slits.

9. Now to apply the rawhide to one of the rounded edges. Fold the rawhide over 1/2" - 1/4" so that you have a smooth edge and begin attaching rawhide to frame with tacks.

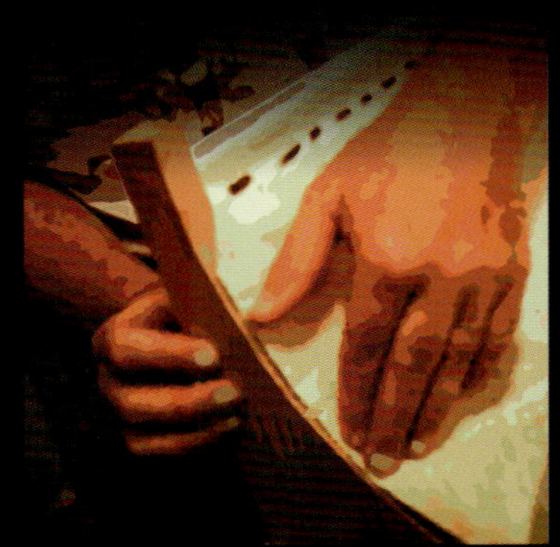

You can use brass, copper, or whatever nail that will not rust. I used brass upholstery tacks. The upholstery tacks bend easily so you have to use a needlenose pliers as a guide or pre-drill very small holes.

Note that the tack is being held by needlenose pliers.

11. Tack down the other rounded edge and you are done.

Glasses Case

If you don't think you're Daniel Boone as far as leathercraft is concerned, then this is the perfect project to get your feet wet on working with rawhide. The directions are straightforward and the entire project can be completed in a short time. One important note is that in the materials it calls for a piece of felt or cotton to use as a liner. Make sure that it is a natural fiber that won't scratch glasses. Many acrylic and other artificial fibers will scratch the lenses on glasses.

Materials

1. One 8" x 8" piece of rawhide

2. An 8" x 8" piece of cotton fabric or light felt

3. A couple feet of stained rawhide lace (see Making Lace pg. 13)

Directions

1. Cut a piece of rawhide according to the illustration (Image 1).

2. Cover the piece of rawhide with mink oil. Really rub it in. Let sit overnight.

3. Wipe off excess mink oil.

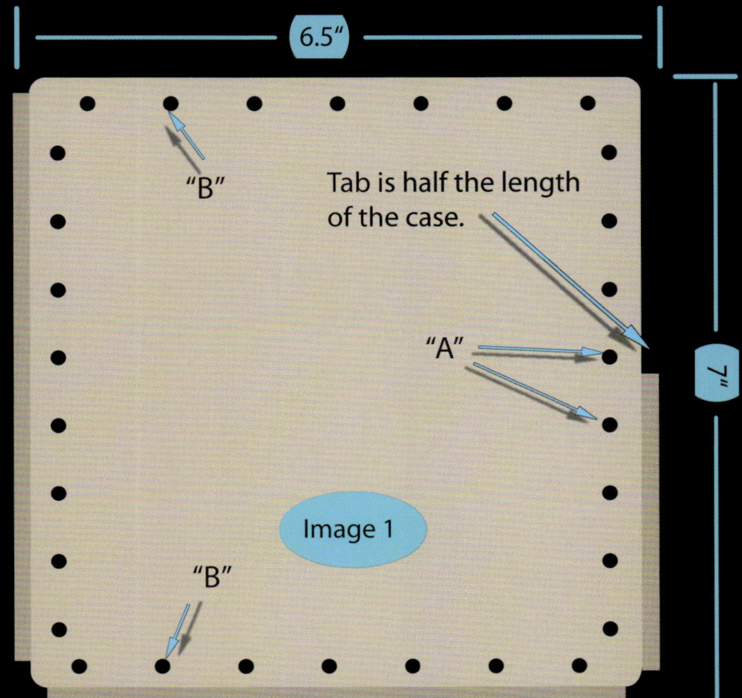

HideCrafts™

Glasses Case

4. Cut your felt or cotton to the size of the rawhide minus the 3/16" tabs (Image 2). The felt liner is held to the inside of the hide with paperclips until lacing is done.

5. Trim the top corners as shown in the illustration.

6. Fold over rawhide as shown in the illustration (Image 3). Do not press the fold so that it leaves a crease. Put a pencil in the middle to avoid this.

7. Fold the rawhide over in half again and this time fold the 3/16" tabs over so that there is a crease. If the rawhide is very stiff, use pliers and a little water to make bends.

8. Using a pencil, draw dots where the holes for the lacing will go. Then using an awl or a power drill, make holes where the dots are.

9. Using your lace, start at the bottom ('A' in Image 1) and sew up to the point where the two sides separate ('B' in illustration) and then sew around the top, finishing back up at point 'B'. This way you will only need one piece of lace.

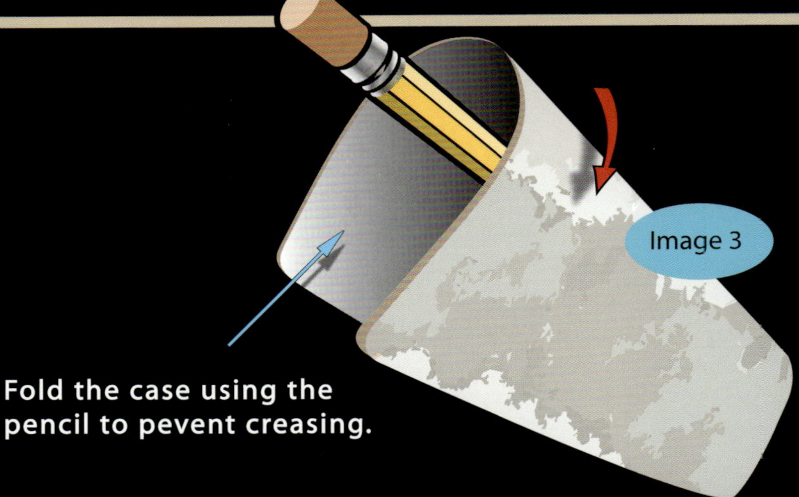

Fold the case using the pencil to pevent creasing.

Fold flaps over with the lining underneath. The lacing will hold the lining in place.

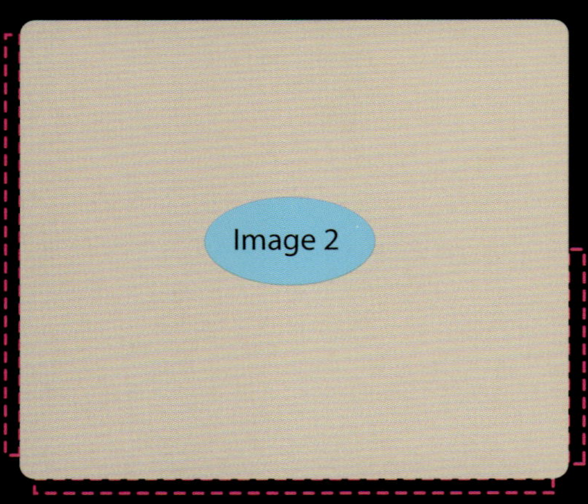

Felt without tab extentions.

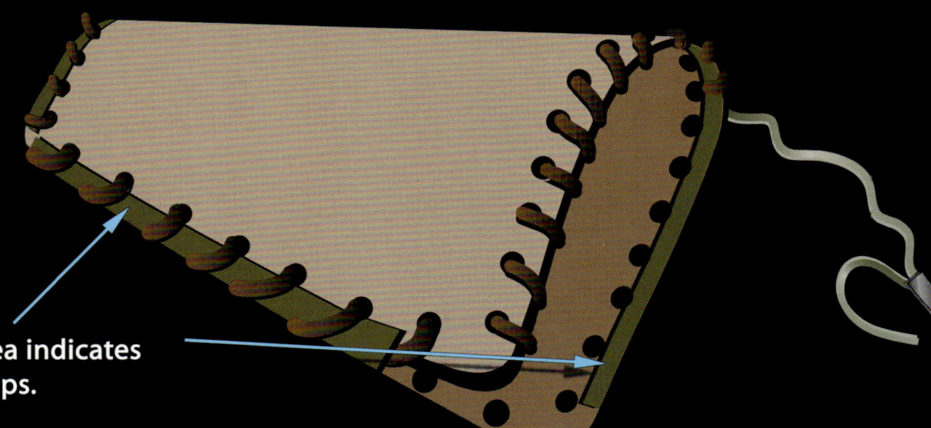

Green area indicates folded flaps.

Knife Sheath

You can make a sheath for your knife or just about any handy tool very easily from a few small pieces of rawhide. In order to hold the two pieces of the project together, I use small rivets which can be purchased at a sewing shop. These rivets hold the rawhide together strongly and also keep the blade from cutting the lace. Also, depending on how thick(or thin) your rawhide is, you might want to double up the thickness of the belt loop part by using two identical pieces of rawhide for the back piece laid on top of each other.

Materials

1. Various pieces of rawhide.

2. Rawhide lace (see Making Lace pg. 13)

3. Eyelet Kit. I used a kit by Dritz which had a tool included.
    A simple hammer was used to punch the tool which then
    closed the eyelet.

4. Button snap from sewing store.

Knife Sheath

Directions

1. Cut the assorted pieces of rawhide as shown in the illustration, using your knife as a model. Leave approximately 1/2" of space around the blade.

2. Place two slight bends around the edge of the two pieces shown in the illustration below. This is to allow space for the blade. Use your fingers to make these bends but if the rawhide is a little tough, use pliers and a little water to achieve this shape.

3. Place outside part (A) over inside part (B). Mark holes 1/4" from edge with pencil, 1/2" apart.

4. The holes in Image 1 will be filled with eyelets where the blade is closest to the edge. You will need 10 - 15 approximately, depending on the size of your blade. Drill holes through both parts and put the eyelets in place and hammer.

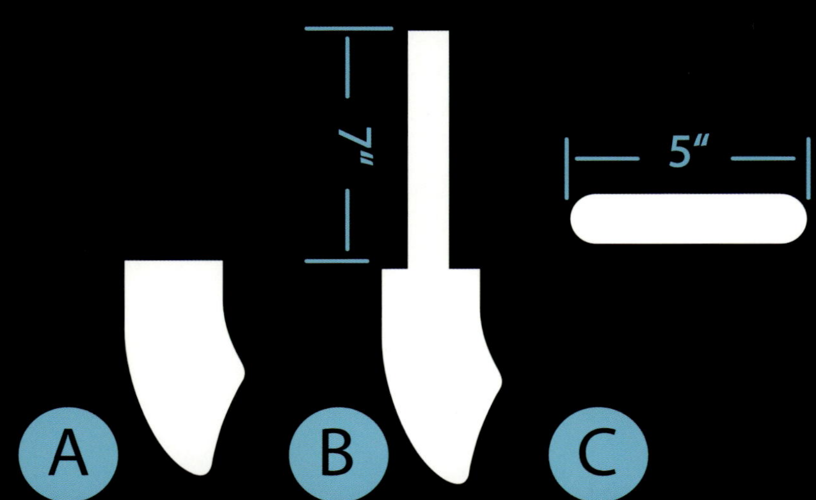

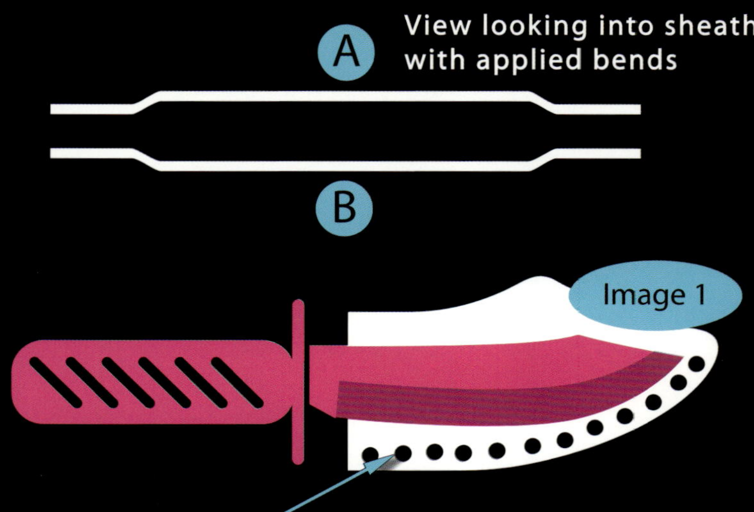

Rivets are placed on the side of the sheath where the sharp edge of the blade rests.

Knife Sheath

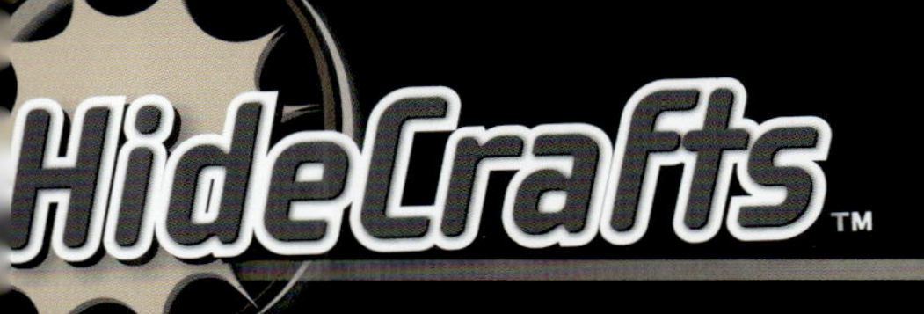

5. Finish the rest of the lacing by cutting holes around the rest of the edge and running lace through the holes & eyelets. See Image 2.

6. Mark and cut holes in belt loop part and run lace through.

7. Bend top of sheath over to make belt loop. Use rawhide to fix loop. See Image 3.

8. Affix snap using an eyelet. Place snap button on each end of strap. See Image 4.

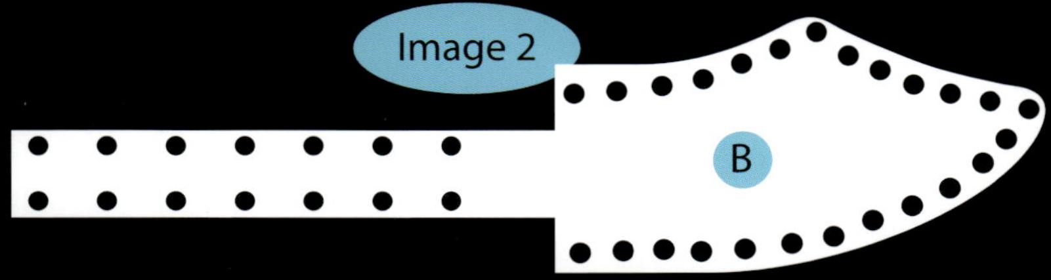
Image 2
B

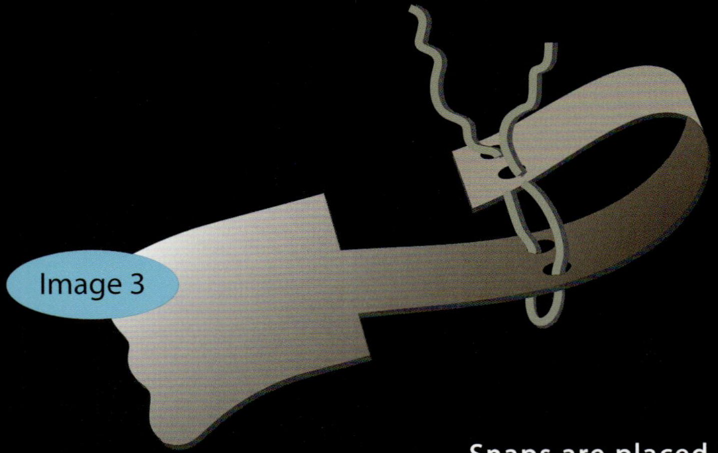
Image 3

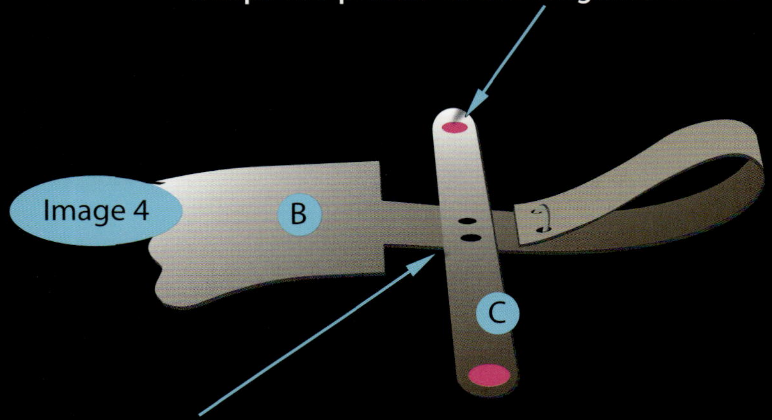
Snaps are placed in the magenta areas
Image 4
B
C
Attach part "C" to part "B" with two metal rivets

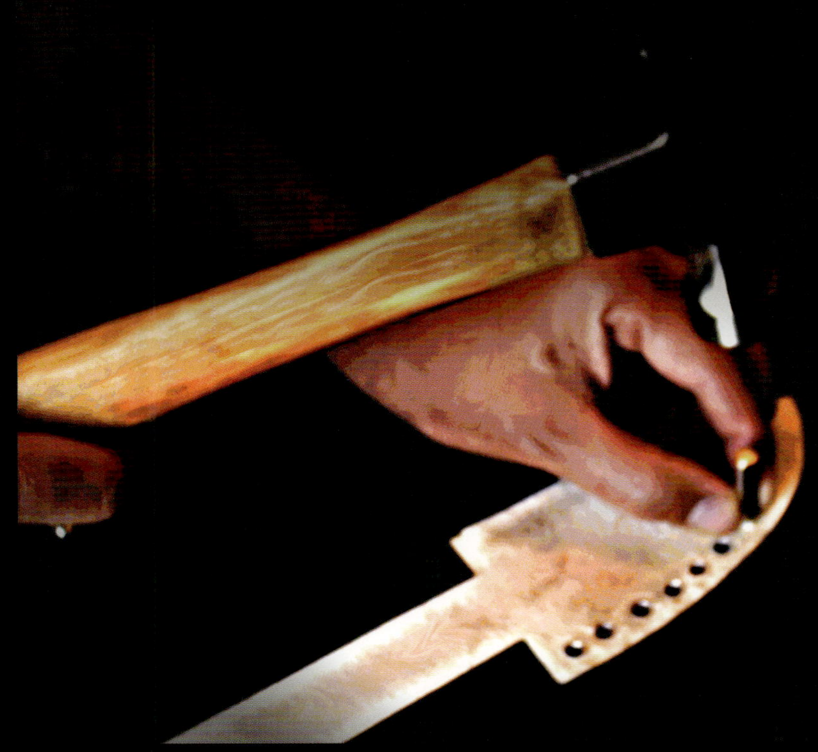

Guitar & Mandolin Strap

I first came across the idea for this strap when I read that a famous country guitarist from the fifties made his own guitar strap from a piece of deer hide. I experimented and found that the dark lace really gave it a striking look, in addition to providing strength. When finished, the strap is stiff yet provides enough bend to be very functional and comfortable. You may have a guitar/mandolin player in your family who would like to have a deerskin strap, too, and this would make a superb gift.

Materials

1. Piece of rawhide roughly 2" x 42". Your length will vary.

2. Two smaller pieces of rawhide about 2" x 6".

3. Plenty of dyed rawhide lace (see Making Lace section pg. 13).

Directions

1. Use a tape measure and your instrument to find a comfortable strap length. Or you can use a strap that you might already have. We'll call your desired length 'X'.

2. Select a width for the strap. For a mandolin strap, the suggested width is 7/8". For a guitar strap, 1 & 1/2" will do. We'll call this 'Y'.

3. Cut a piece of rawhide as shown in the illustration. Length will be 'X' and width will be (2 x 'Y') + 3/16". See illustration for actual size of ends of strap.

4. Cut the two end pieces as shown in the illustration.

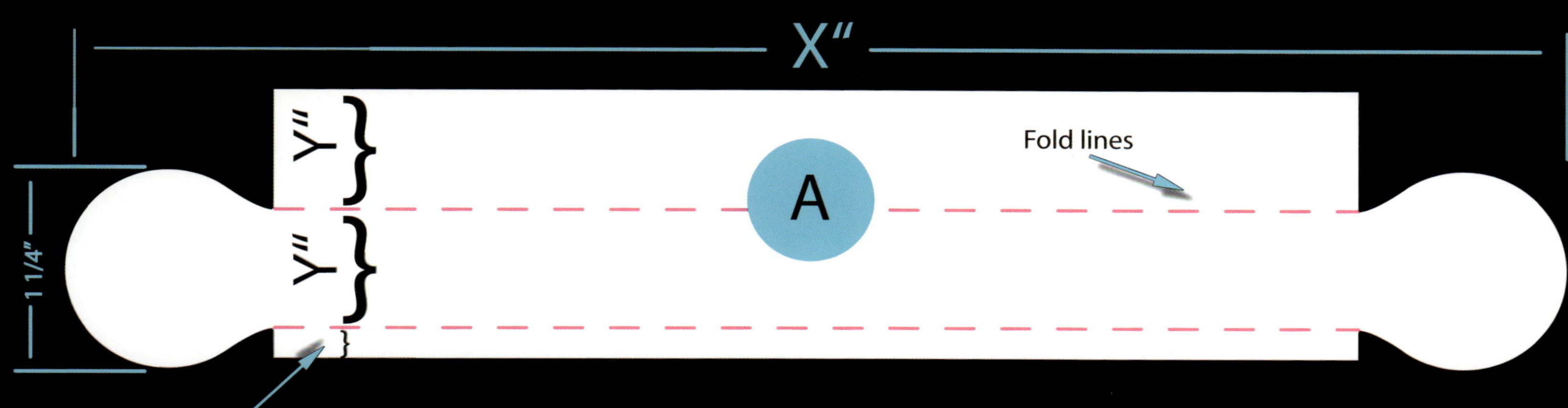

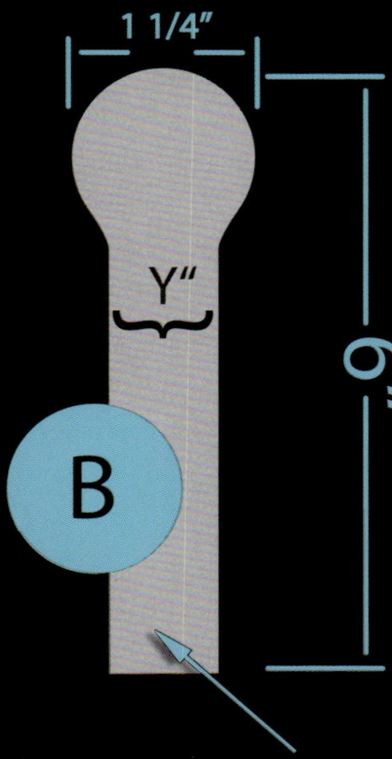

5. If you haven't already done so, prepare the rawhide as per the instructions (see Hide Preparation section), and coat both sides of rawhide pieces with a liberal amount of mink oil. Really rub it in. Leave it sit overnight and wipe off excess the next day.

6. Now fold over the dotted lines as shown in the illustration. If your rawhide is still fairly stiff, use pliers to help you get a nice fold. If it starts to crack a little during folding, apply more mink oil to it.

7. Put the two end pieces in place so that they fit inside the folded main part and the rounded ends are matching. These two pieces are there to provide extra strength where the strap clips on to the instrument.

1 1/4"
Y"
6"
B

Make two of these reinforcement pieces.

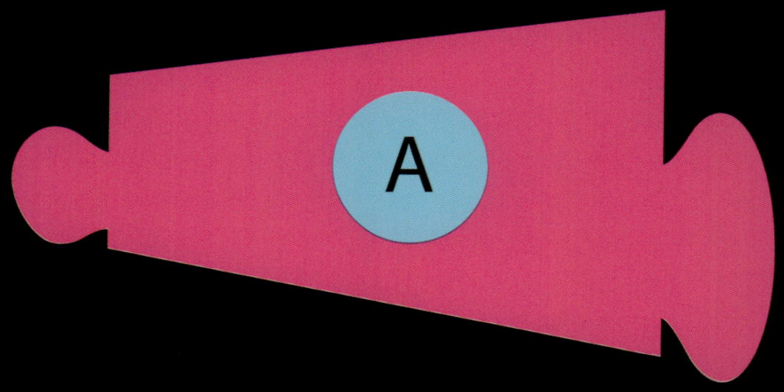

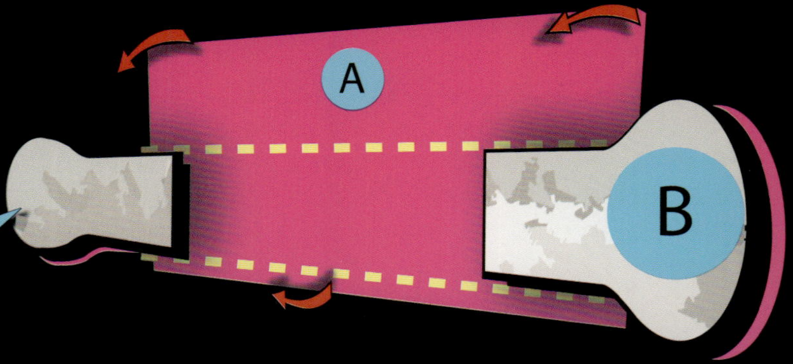

The reinforcement pieces; As attached to "A".

Put the two "B" tabs (reinforcement pieces) on the "A" piece as seen below.

A

A

B

Fold "A" at the dotted line over the "B" tabs, with the 3/16 folded last.

Guitar & Mandolin Strap

Mark for holes with a pencil and then drill or punch.

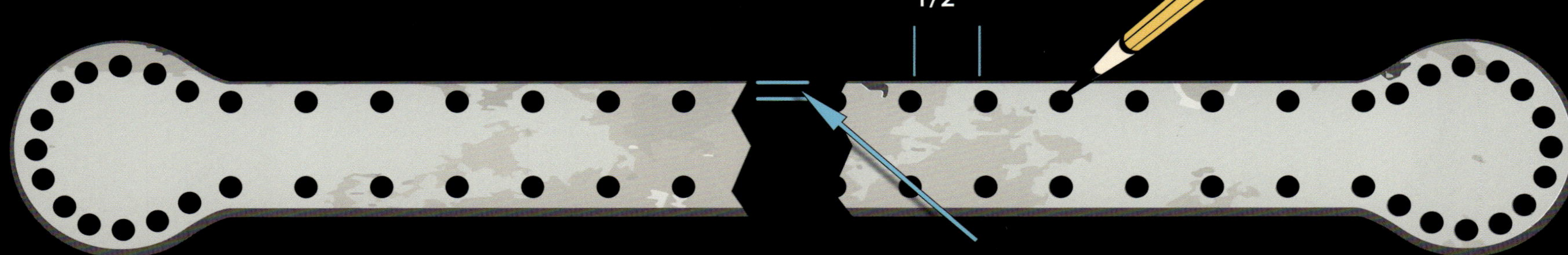

8. Using a ruler and following the illustration, put pencil marks every 1/2", making sure they are 3/16" from the edge, all of the way around. This will be where the holes go for the lace. Using either an awl or a power drill, make holes where you put your pencil marks.

9. Using your stained lace (see Making Lace section), sew the edges as shown in the illustration. When you come to the end of a piece of lace, thin it down some and tie the next piece of lace to it, trying to get the knot on the back side of the strap.

10. Now to make the hole for the guitar button. Drill two holes in the end pieces and cut on the dotted lines as shown in illustration "A". You may have to make yours a little smaller or bigger depending on the size of your button.

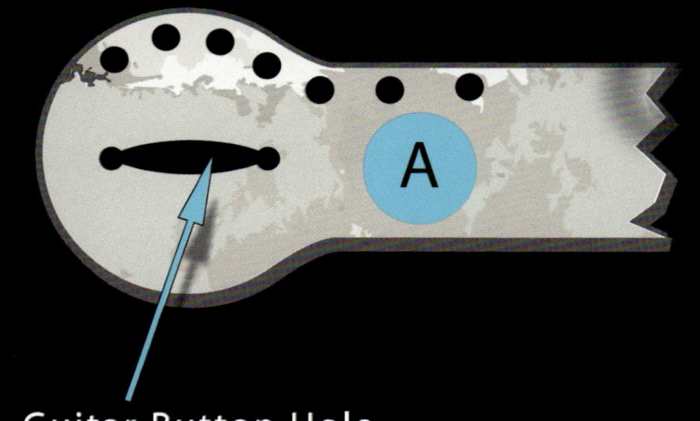

Guitar Button Hole

Lacing seen from the back of strap.

This is a detail of the strap fixed on the button at the bottom of the mandolin.

This practice quiver is a lightweight handy piece of archery equipment. The flat wooden bottom gives it a sturdy base and the hole and strap allow you to carry it or hang it from a hook in the garage or closet when not being used. When you want to set up and practice shooting at the deer target in the yard, you can stand up the quiver by putting a stake or old arrow in the ground and put the two rings on the side of the quiver through the stake.

Materials

1. Piece of rawhide 19" x 20"

2. Plenty of rawhide lace (see Making Lace pg. 13).

3. Two metal rings about 3/4" in diameter. Keyrings work fine.

4. One 6" x 6" x 1/2" piece of hardwood. I used hard maple scrap from a lumber store.

5. Brass or copper tacks, about 3/8" long. These can be bought at most hardware stores.

Directions

1. Cut a piece of hide in a rectangular shape roughly 19" x 20"

2. Using an awl (or power drill), cut holes every 3/4" as in the illustration. There should be three rows of holes, the row on the left being 1/2" from the left edge, the middle row being 2 & 1/4" from the right edge, and the right row being 1 & 3/4" from the right edge.

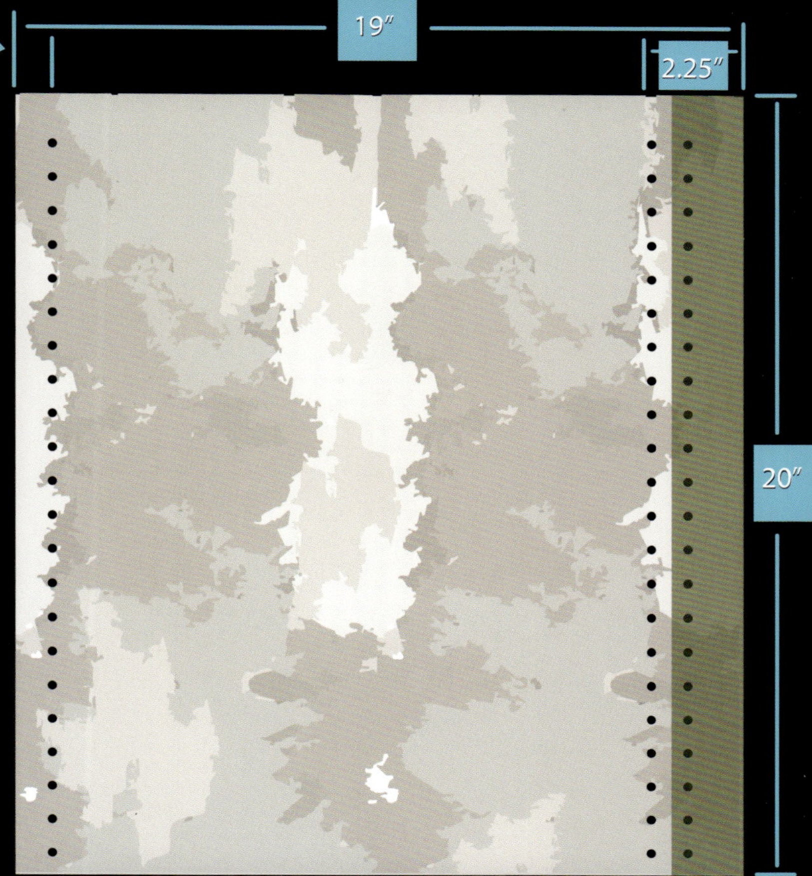

Deer Hide Practice Quiver

3. Bend the hide and make a tube so that the shaded area (Image 3) is inside the tube.

4. Using your rawhide lace, sew the piece together, adding the metal rings to the middle and at the bottom.

5. Now for the top. Fold over the top 1/4"edge of the tube and make holes with awl (or drill) every 1/2" just below the folded edge. Sew with lace. At the point where the two pieces overlap, trim outer 1/4" of tube.

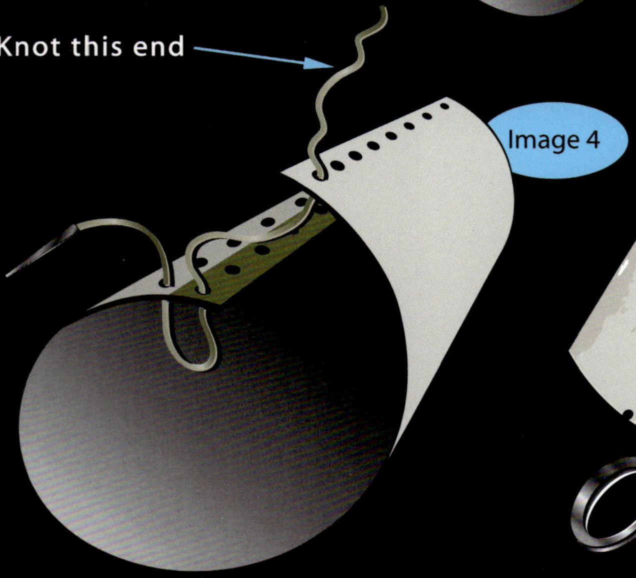

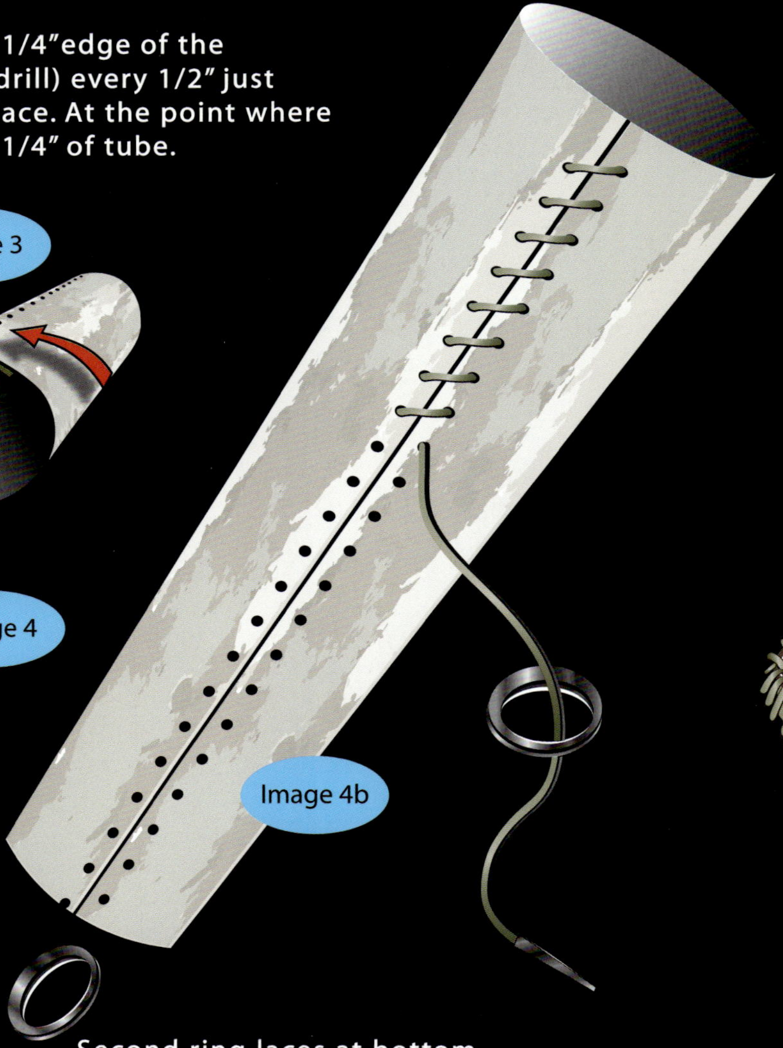

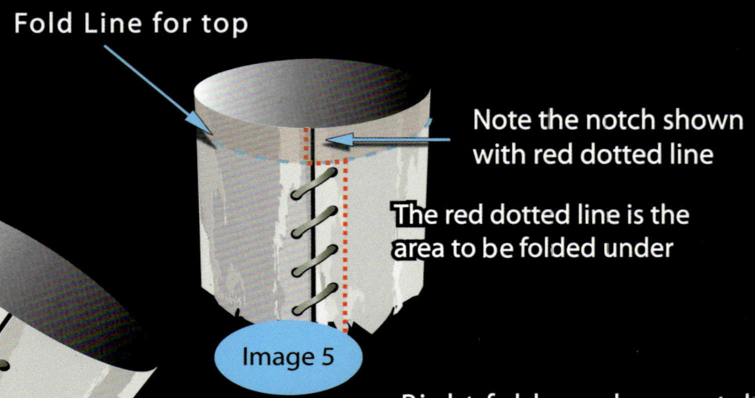

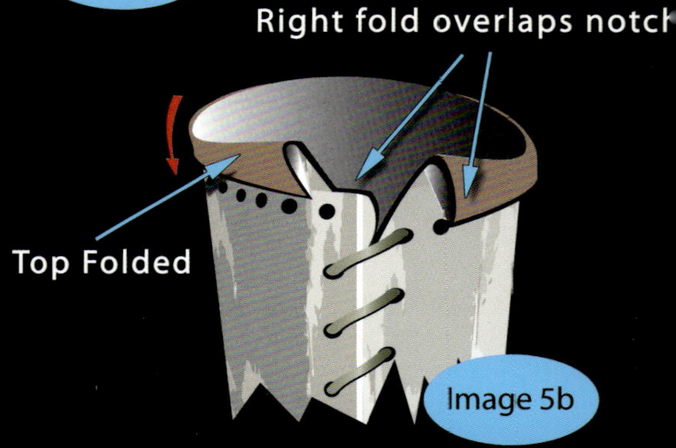

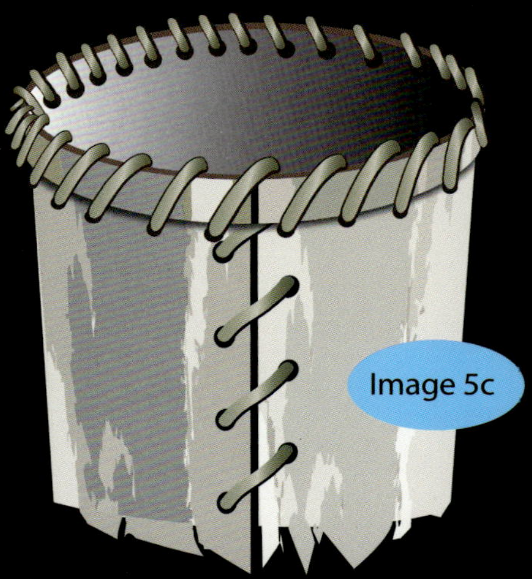

6. Find the appropriate diameter of the bottom of the tube. From your 6" x 6" piece of hardwood, cut a circle with that diameter.

7. Place the hardwood disc in the tube at the bottom and, using your brass or copper nails, hammer the disc in place with a nail every 1 & 1/2".

8. Using a small wooden stick (or an old broken arrow), you can stand up your quiver in the yard when you practice. You can also add a string(or rawhide braided rope)for carrying by cutting a hole near the top and putting the rope through.

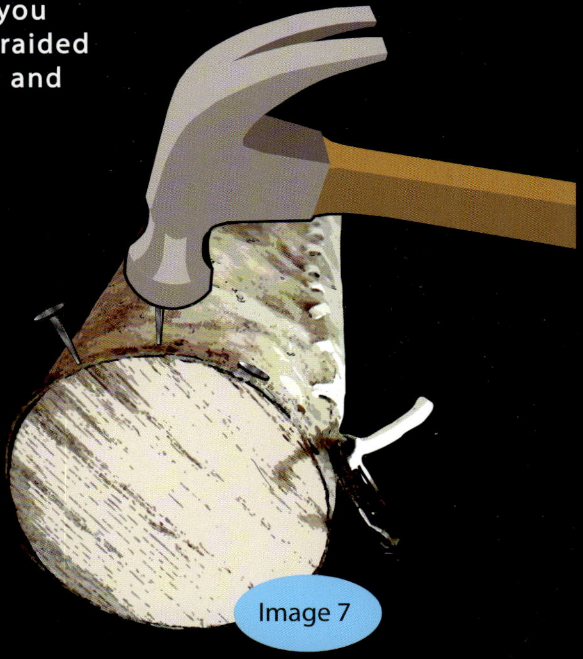

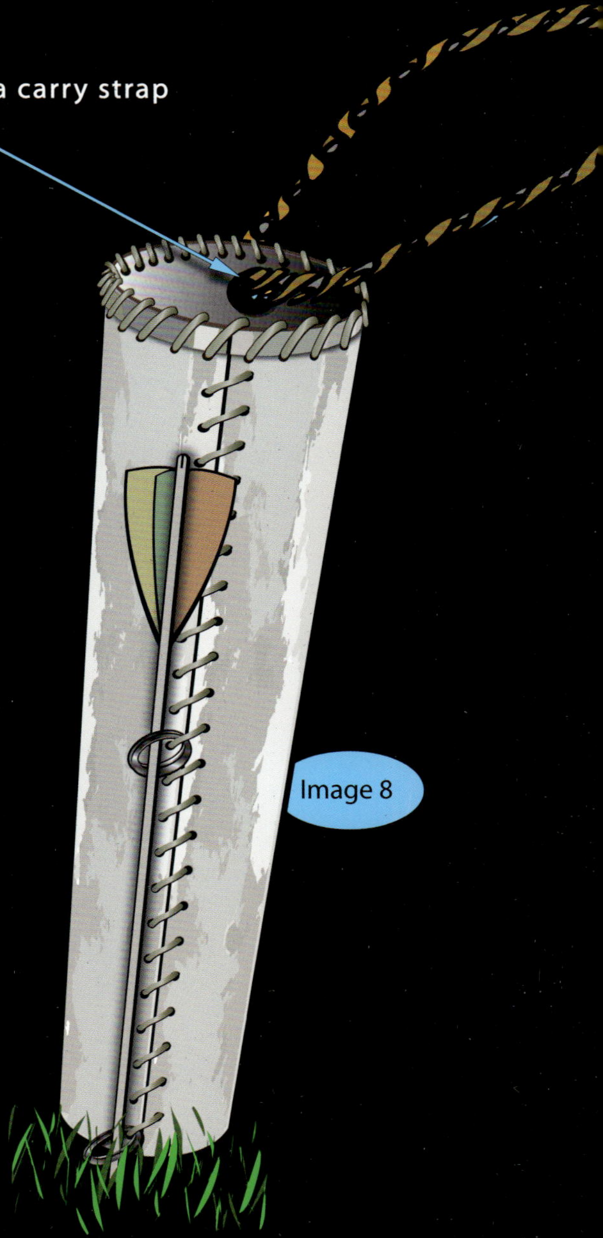

Optional 3/4" hole for a carry strap

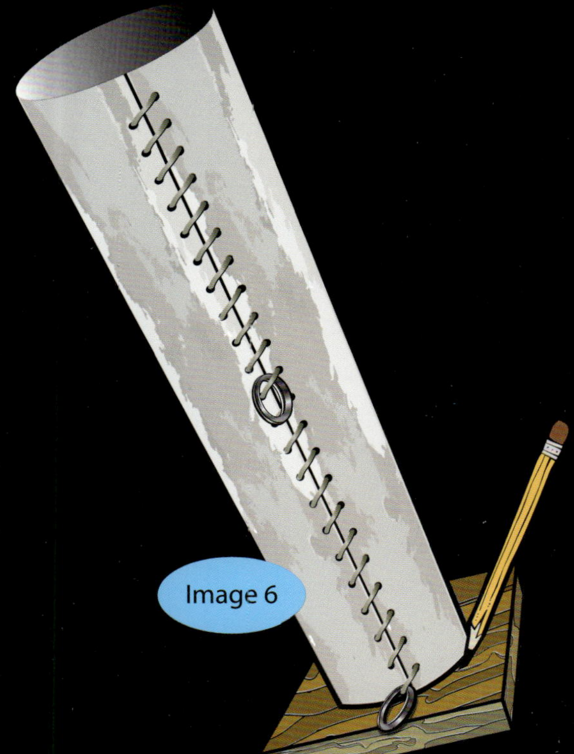

Image 6

Image 7

Image 8